101 TC
FC
PHD STUDENTS

Professor IAIN H WOODHOUSE

MAY 2015

SPECKLED PRESS

Copyright © Iain H Woodhouse 2015

First drafted 2014

CONTENTS

Preface

Thank you to all the PhD students I've supervised who have helped me learn these things. I did not do many of them myself. In fact, this is the book I wish I'd had when I started. It is said that "Advice is a form of nostalgia," so forgive me if some of it seems nostalgic. I have, however, tried to refrain from that kind of advice and instead I've gone for a checklist approach — a practical toolbox of stuff that you can actually use. And hopefully a bit of fun too.

And thank you also to those people who gave me feedback and helped improve the text: David Morrison, Katrin Loer, and especially Karen MacIntyre.

Before you start

1. Ask yourself: Why do I want to do a PhD?

The answer is important. It will help guide you to the right location and help you ask a potential supervisor the right questions. If you find that question too abstract, then try an alternative: "Where do I want my PhD to take me?" Keep asking these questions.

2. Choose the right institution (for you).

Let's be frank: there is a snobbery about institutions. Getting your PhD from the "right" institution for your subject can set you up for life. But be careful, as some institutions have reputations that far outshine their actual performance. It is easy to find stories of students at prestigious universities who had a dreadful time — it is equally easy to find success stories at institutions that otherwise would be considered below-par.

But the fact of the matter is that, all else considered, the former will always have an easier time when it comes to finding a job, well after that first post-doc. It would be nice if the world wasn't like that, but it is. Of course, everyone has individual stories, and you might find that for your particular circumstances, your options are limited. Family commitments, relationships, hobbies, should all factor into your decision as well, but if you do have a choice, then consider the options carefully. Perhaps much more important than the institution's broader reputation is the standing of the specific department or unit or group where you will do the PhD. The best place to study the subject of your PhD may not be located within the highest-ranking institutions. This is especially the case if you plan to have an academic career in the subject of your PhD, since those "in the know" know all too well which departments are the best. How can you know too?

- **Ask your current tutor, or lecturer**. When you go to a PhD interview, you can also subtly ask them. "If I graduate here, where else might employ me?" is a question you might ask your panel, for instance.

- **Look at the high achievers in the field**. Who is being asked to give keynotes at conferences? Who is publishing the key papers or books? Look at where they are now, but also look at where they graduated. A biography in a journal paper or book should tell you even if their website doesn't.

- **League tables can help**, but I wouldn't use it to make final decisions, and I wouldn't get too pernickety about the exact placing in the table. Use other indicators such as publications (you will be able to access publication databases in your current institution), or check the main funding bodies for annual reports to see how much research funding each institution wins compared to others.

- **Visit the place**. Actually walking the corridors and meeting the staff will make a huge difference to how you feel about an institution. It might even override all of the above points. Getting a feel for the wider geographic context is also important (which is where all those personal factors might also come into play).

3. Choose the right topic.

It may be that you choose your topic first, and then seek out the right place to do it, or vice versa. But at some point you have to hone in on a topic. Choose one that suits you. Be fussy. You will be expected to commit 3-4 years of your life to this topic and devote more energy and enthusiasm to it than possibly anything else in your entire life (expect, perhaps, children or maybe a start-up company!). It will potentially shape your whole career because your PhD both defines your area of expertise but also channels you into a particular community of people working on similar topics.   It is therefore a good idea to get it right. Unfortunately, I have no clever tactics to help you choose it, other than to encourage you to read. Read widely on the subjects that interest you and all the subjects around that subject. Then read some more. Read books and monographs, but especially read the peer-reviewed literature (some of which is now available as open-access, so you don't need to be at a university already to be able to read it). If you are still not sure, then maybe you need to take some more time to decide on doing a PhD. If you haven't done so already, studying a Masters degree is sometimes a good opportunity to test the water, so to speak. Indeed, some PhD programmes insist on studying a Masters prior to beginning your PhD.

The PhD topic is supposed to be original, and being up to date on the literature will help you get a sense for whether or not your proposal is original enough. In general, though, I would expect your potential supervisor to help — if not at the application stage, then certainly after you have started.

4. Choose the right supervisor.

PhDs are sometimes conducted in groups or labs. Sometimes they are conducted in dark lonely corners. In both cases, the one person you really need to get on with is your supervisor. I would be very cautious about starting a PhD with a supervisor you have never met, or at least not without first-hand testimony from others who have known them. Normally your supervisor will want to meet you too, before taking you on, but not always (especially in the case of international applications).

5. Funding.

Sometimes, you won't have the luxury of choosing your topic, and instead your topic will be chosen for you. A fully funded PhD scholarship is, for many, too good an opportunity to miss, but often this comes with the downside of being tied to a topic that is already very well defined. It may also be tied to a particular business sector, or come from a source that has particular political leanings. In such cases, you may want to consider if you will be comfortable relying on this source for your income for 3-5 years, and potentially influencing your entire future career. If you have done (1)-(4) above and thought about this thoroughly, it should at least be easier for you to match any available funded PhD topics to the ones that interest you.

Getting The Right Mindset

6. Plan.

I know some of you won't like the idea of planning research. Surely research should be free to roam where the results lead you. You can't plan that. But that is not the kind of planning I mean. What I am referring to is knowing what needs to be done, mapping the steps that will achieve those things, and pre-empting some of the obstacles that will hinder you on your path to successful completion of your PhD. You will have heard stories of (or indeed, know some) final year PhDs working all hours available to them, and then some. Most PhD candidates don't submit in the allotted time. The likely reason for these scenarios is that they didn't plan. In a PhD, the planning process is relatively straightforward to start because you know what result you are trying to achieve — a successful PhD submission. You can then set a time by which you aim to achieve this. Choose a sensible time, noting key events such as when your funding runs out, when your supervisor does most of their teaching, or when they take their holidays. Choose an actual day as your deadline for submission and work backwards.

When you are planning, think of it as if you were trying to get across a river. You know what it is you wish to achieve — to get to the other side without getting wet. We note the length of our stride (no point placing stones too far apart). We work out the distance across the river. Then we choose a suitable place to cross. To achieve this you must place out a sequence of stepping stones that get you to your goal. So, we must first take note of how many stones we have and their size and shape. The planning is the process by which we choose how best to place each stone. The next stage is to act — that is, actually crossing the river. Now, I'm guessing you have never done a PhD before, so it may take you some time to learn the "length of your stride" or to judge the distance to the other bank. This comes with time and experience, so be prepared to always adjust your plan to match your own skill set and your style of getting things done.

7. Act.

Planning is only part of the process. You need to stick to your plan. Your plan can change, indeed it should change: "No plan survives first contact with the enemy," is a quotation I often use (attributed to Helmuth von Moltke, a 19th century German Field Marshall). As you act out your plan, circumstances change, unexpected things happen, and things don't always go according to plan. This is normal. You need to constantly evolve you plan, adjust the stepping stones and modify your path across the river. It is knowing the end result that allows you to adjust your plan but stay on track to achieving it. By following your plan, you will also have a better idea of whether you are on schedule or not.

8. Be SMART.

SMART is an acronym for

> Specific
>
> Measurable
>
> Achievable
>
> Results-oriented.
>
> Time-bound

When you set out your plan for your PhD, use SMART language for your goals — your stepping stones.

Not being specific means being woolly and vague. You wouldn't want to do that in your actual thesis, so why do it in your plan?

If you can't measure (in a very general sense of the word) a each step in your plan, then how do you know when you have achieved them? How will you know you are "on track"?

Without a very specific goal, how will you know if it can be achieved in the available time or with the available resources?

Is the purpose of this stepping stone sufficiently clear? What result are you looking for by achieving this task?

Have you constrained the time scale? By when, exactly (to at least the nearest day), must this be task be completed in order to stay on schedule?

Let's look at an example: *Review the topic of X.*

This is not a SMART task because it is not specific enough (what elements of X are you reviewing?), it is not measurable (how do you know when you have completed this task?), it is not results oriented (what is the purpose of the review?) and it is not time-bound (by when does this need to be completed?). It is not clear if it is achievable or not because it is too vague.   Here are some SMARTer versions of the same goal:

By 21st December, comprehensively review (with no less than 40 relevant articles) the development of topic X since 1960, with special emphasis on how the methodologies have evolved so that I can justify the methods I will employ in my own work.   Is it clearer what this task now involves? Is it now easier to define the time commitment? Will it be clearer when this task is complete?   Is this goal easier to plan for, rather than simply Review the topic of X ?

Your reaction to planning out these tasks in detail will vary greatly, depending on your culture, your approach to getting things done, and your track record (people who consider themselves sufficiently successful, or "successful enough" rarely want to change their habits).   Some of you will have the luxury of PhD funding that has no end-point, and an institution that doesn't demand you submit your thesis within a particular time window. If that is you, great. You are free to meander aimlessly through your intellectual pursuits until you discover a conclusion to your PhD.   Unfortunately, this is not a luxury afforded to most PhD scholars these days, and if you want to finish on time, within budget, and (relatively) stress free, then I recommend learning how to plan your time. All things being equal, my money is on the student who learns how to both plan and act on that plan.

9. Read up on impostor syndrome.

Sometimes you may feel out of your depth. Good. That suggests you are at the right institution. It also suggests you are learning. It takes quite a substantial amount of knowledge about a subject to be able to recognise you are out of your depth. I tended to find this whenever I tried to learn a language: the simple pleasantries and functional parts of a language would seem quite easy to learn. And then I would learn enough to start to realise how much more there was to learn. The thing to remember is that you have to learn quite a bit before you can see how much you still have to learn.

But you do need to know whether you just have impostor syndrome or if you really are out of your depth. Symptoms of impostor syndrome include:

- Starting to wonder if your supervisor made a mistake in taking you on for a PhD in the first place;
- Starting to see everyone else around you as cleverer and more capable than you;
- Feeling reluctant to speak up in groups of your peers or staff for fear that everyone else will think you are stupid for asking such a silly question.

Apparently, women are more prone to impostor syndrome, but everyone can suffer from it at some point in their life.   Being amongst a group of high-achieving academics would surely be voted "place most likely to prompt feelings of inadequacy"! There are plenty of tips online about how to address this syndrome, but the important thing for you is to be able to tell the difference between this (which probably isn't a problem) and actually being inadequate (which may well be a problem). Meeting all the benchmarks in the PhD programme is one way to tell you are not an imposter. Writing a paper for a conference or a journal as soon as you can, as this is also a good indicator.   Remember, within the entire group of PhD candidates in your Department/School/Unit, you can expect that about half of you are below average. Do not let it worry you if you are in the bottom half. It doesn't mean you can't still make it.   As a general rule, if you were honest in your application process, then you should be fine. And if in doubt, ask your supervisor.

10. Don't panic. Ever.

Seek help. Remember what Dumbledore said about Hogwarts and apply to your own institution: "Help will always be given at [insert name of your university] to those who ask for it." Even if it is not your supervisor, I pretty much guarantee that your university has someone who is both willing and able to help you overcome whatever obstacles are thrown in your path. Sometimes this will be your supervisor, but often they are neither qualified nor mandated to help, and their primary role is to point you to the right people within the institution. Additionally, talk to other students. Talk to other people generally. Ask more experienced students or staff about their experiences. Is this normal? Did this ever happen to you? What did you do in those circumstances?

11. Anticipate that your morale will reach an all-time low about two thirds of the way through your thesis.

This is normal. Many years ago I heard about studies conducted to evaluate the morale and psychological well-being of participants engaged in some task. I remember it as being a NASA study for long term missions, but I now can't find a reference other than to some work on soldiers. The results showed that morale reached the lowest point about 2/3 of the way through the task. It didn't matter how long the mission lasted, it was always 2/3. I've seen this happen to countless PhD students and it also happened to me as a student. So for a 3 or 4 year PhD, at about end of year 2, or first half of year 3, respectfully, you can anticipate that you will have a serious low point. You will wonder if you will ever get the darn thing finished on time. You will question the quality of the work. You will chastise yourself for not having worked as hard as you should have done in the first 60% of the PhD. You may even question why you ever decided to embark on a PhD in the first place.

All this is perfectly normal. Accept it as the lowest point. Seek out people who will spend time listening to you. Take advantage of your university student counselling service, if talking about it with a stranger helps you get through this trough (sometimes it is easier talking to someone you don't know).

For some of you, the best way to plod your way through this will be to set out micro-steps of progress. Find tiny tasks that have clear outcomes and are well-defined in time, so that you keep moving forwards, even if it is very slowly. It will definitely help at this stage if you have been rigorous with your task planning. If you have a detailed plan already, you can start to pick out tasks that are methodical and functional, rather than tasks that require lots of brain power. Things such as getting references together into a database, or improving your diagrams, are the kind of tasks that work well. If your plan includes a set of SMART tasks (as it should) look for some of the less taxing ones, and bring them forward if you have to.

Above all, don't panic. Seek advice. Talk to people. Keep moving forwards, even if it is only by tiny steps. And if none of the above works at this point, then take a break. It is always possible to shuffle your plan around to make room for a week or two to go away — indeed, if you really need a break, feel confident that you can always adjust the plan when you get back. (Of course, if you have been keeping up to date with your planning you will already know that there is room for a break). Visit family or friends. Talk. Walk. Swim. Indulge in fresh air and get some perspective.

12. Make yourself easy to help.

You will find, in your PhD as in life, that people are more likely to give you help if you make it easy for them to do so. This applies especially to your supervisor. If you are based in a laboratory, or in some distinct team, your supervisor may always be around to help. In other cases, you may have to work hard to find your supervisor — they are busy people, after all. So when you need help, make it clear that you need help and approach the problem in a solution-focused way. If you go to your supervisor and say, "I have this problem, I wonder if I should do A or B, or perhaps even do C. What do you think?" you are more likely to get a quick answer than if you ask the open question: "I have this problem, can you help." The latter question is sometimes the right one to ask, but it is harder to provide a quick answer.

Perhaps the time you might need most help is in those rare occasions when you fall out with your supervisor. In that case it is quite definitely a good idea to approach the problem with a clear idea of what you would like as a solution. You can then approach other members of academic staff, or support staff, and seek help. Of course, they should be very supportive and willing to help, but the clearer you make your request for a solution, the easier it will be for them to help.

Being Effective

Self-Improvement

It is very likely that the following tips are things that you know already. You maybe learned this as an undergraduate, or maybe you always had these skills. I include them here for completeness, for those people who need a reminder.

13. Learn new skills.

Universities offer many opportunities to learn something new. Learn a new language. Improve an existing one. Learn to write computer code. Improve your writing skills or your presentation skills. Learning something new helps to break the intensity (monotony?) of the thesis topic, but also adds something valuable to your personal resources. For me, it was memory systems. I was always very poor at remembering names of authors, or the formulation of key physical relationships. I was sure I understood it all at the time, but had a hard time remembering everything that I felt I needed to know. So I sought out a book from the library (I'm showing my age now!) about memory systems. I can't remember now what it was called... sorry, just kidding — it was The Memory Book by Harry Lorayne. I still use the systems, although not as often as I should, but I am pretty sure that I improved significantly at the time. Your memory is maybe just fine, in which case you might consider learning how to touch-type, or speed-read, or mind-map, or just about anything that you think will improve your ability to get things done. Universities often provide free courses on many of these kinds of generic skills, so I recommend you consider finding at least one that you can focus on improving while you do your PhD. Since it will also give you break from your thesis topic, there is no real down side.

14. Join a club or society.

As with the last tip, there are potential new skills to be learnt in a student society, but a society should also include a more social side. Meet some like-minded people. Better still, meet some people who don't think like you. Expand your social horizons. Meet people outside of your discipline. You might include volunteering in this category. There are always charities looking for willing volunteers to contribute some time.

15. Play.

A sport, a hobby, a favourite computer game. Having fun outside your PhD environment is important.

16. Eat Properly.

Being unhealthy is not conducive to doing a good PhD. There are usually inexpensive ways to eat good, fresh produce in a University town. Ask someone to give you a good cookbook for your next Christmas/Birthday present.

17. Exercise.

Exercise is part of the healthy lifestyle. No need to go to the gym, but make sure you walk instead of taking the bus; use the stairs instead of the lift/escalator. Cycle. Run. Dance. And make sure you take regular breaks from the computer. You can now get software that will remind you when you have been sitting at your computer for too long. I have one that I have set to tell me to take a 10 min break after ever 50 mins of working on my computer. Sometimes I ignore it. But usually I do try to stand up, stretch, walk around, or just generally do something other than sitting staring at a screen.

18. Keep your perspective.

You already know what things make you *you* but the intensity of a PhD may cause you to forget it sometimes. Your PhD is not the most important thing in the world. Don't worry about occasionally spending time wandering aimlessly. Your health, your sanity, your friends, your family, your relationships, are all more important than your thesis. That is not a reason to give up when things get difficult, but rather a reminder to prioritise your life.

Time management

19. You cannot really "manage" time.

But you can learn to manage yourself more effectively, and improve the way you prioritise what you spend your time doing. This is one skill that you might get an opportunity to improve and will definitely make you more effective in the long run. Here are some key tips on learning the art of "time":

a) **Take command of your diary.** Whether it is a physical diary or an electronic one, make sure it is you who is in charge of it, not other people. What I mean by that is that you need to fill it with *your* priorities first, before it gets filled up with other people's demands. So, first fill it with allocated times for the tasks you need to complete to meet your own schedule (NB: if you have planned things out well from following Tip 6, then you know what needs to be done by when). Only then do you consider the invitations, meetings, requests for appointments, or other events that *other people* want to put into your diary. If you haven't filled your diary with the stuff that you need to do, you will incorrectly look at your diary and say "Yes, I'm free," whenever anyone else asks for your time. But you are only really free if you have factored in the activities you need to do to keep on schedule. This is the reason why, at the planning stage, you should remember to include flexibility for unanticipated events that have to fitted into the schedule somewhere.   It also means you should factor in time off: holidays, parties, festivals, hobbies, etc.

b) **Never go into a meeting without knowing when it is going to end.** If it doesn't say it on the agenda, then ask before the meeting. If you don't ask before the meeting, ask it of the chair as soon as you arrive at the meeting. You are then free to leave the meeting when the end time arrives. If the meeting goes on beyond the scheduled end time, you should not feel obliged to stay. And you needn't feel awkward or guilty about doing so. (If you need to leave before the end of the scheduled end time, let the chair know before the meeting starts.)

c) **Learn to say, "no".**   There is a great quote from Benjamin Franklin: "If you want something done ask a busy person." He is referring to the fact that busy people are "doers" — they get off their butt and do stuff.   But you might also wonder if the reason these busy people are doing stuff (especially if they are doing it for other people) is because they are suffering from the *yes-disease* — that uncontrollable urge to say "yes" whenever anyone asks you to do something for them.

Working on Your Network

20. Join LinkedIn and Research Gate...

...or whichever platforms are popular when you are reading this. Whatever these platforms evolve into, it will definitely becoming increasingly important for you to be visible on these network tools. There are three ways you can use Linkedin which I believe will be of value to you: as a contacts database, a connection tracker and a grouping tool. And if you are worried about it taking up too much time, try factoring it (and the other things below) into your plan by allocating a small amount of time each week to deal with these things.

a) **Managing your address book**: An especially useful thing about LinkedIn is that it is not just a social networking tool – it's a dynamic address book. My mobile phone's Linkedin App synchronises with my online connections, so if someone links to me, all the contact information they have volunteered on their profile (including their photo) is automatically added to my address book. It is now quite normal to invite someone to connect via Linkedin if you swap business cards with them.

b) **Tracking your network**: Not only are you able to have the contact information of people you know/work with/studied with/etc, but the information will always be up to date (if they are maintaining their profile). Where they now work, and who they are connected to. Keeping up-to-date on who is doing what is potentially valuable when you start looking for jobs, or seeking out collaborators for grant applications. You will also be able to tap into your supervisor's network. One of the most valuable things your supervisor can offer you is access to their address book, and Linkedin does just that.

c) **Groups**: Joining groups, or setting up your own group, provides you with a place for discussion, news, jobs and product or service promotions. Depending on the individual's settings, you can also contact people in your network. Your undergraduate or postgraduate institutions, or the institution where you are doing your PhD, will also have alumni groups. Join them.

d) **Word of warning**: I thoroughly recommend using Linkedin as a contacts database. But just as you can keep tabs on your network, so your network can keep tabs on you. Seven people viewed my profile last week. It's therefore important that if you join Linkedin you keep track of what you are sharing. I have a simple model: my Linkedin profile is my professional persona, fully open to the public and nothing about my personal life. My Facebook profile is my private life. The other warning is not to get sucked into the whole social networking shenanigans. All the above you can do very quickly if you put your mind to it, but it's also very easy to get completely absorbed with the lives of other people.

21. Start blogging.

Even if that is a basic blog where you simply comment occasionally on news items in your field of study. If you sync your blog to your Facebook, Twitter and Linkedin accounts, you will find you can populate all of them by simply populating one of them. The advantage of writing a blog is threefold:

a) It will help you **find your "voice"**. If your PhD is in a technical subject you may not have written very much prose in your studies to date. Writing a blog will improve your writing skills. It will help you get used to writing "for a reader" rather than simply "as a record". Your final thesis will benefit from all the practice you will get from writing a blog.

b) **Findability**. When you apply for a job there is a good chance your potential employers will search for you on the internet. You want them to find good things about you. A well-populated, even if out-of-date, blog will have a high chance of being found (blog platforms are good at their search engine optimisation) and will express who you are better than your CV.

c) **Sharing your work.** Many people either

won't access your publications and conference proceedings (because they are lazy or they aren't aware of your work) or they can't access them (because they are behind a paywall). Blogging gives you the chance to talk more informally about your research, to share your work more easily, and effectively promote yourself as researcher. In this way your blog may be more like a place to host copies (and lay person summaries) of your research papers and posters — it doesn't have to be a regular column with weekly/monthly commentary.

22. Take every opportunity to meet new people.

Every new person you meet is a potential future collaborator, customer, employer, employee, friend. Every time you are forced to sit next to a stranger (planes, trains, boats, conference dinners, weddings), give yourself the task of finding out which one of these they might be.   Say hello. Swap business cards. When travelling to conferences, talk to the people next to you on the plane, or train, or taxi, or whatever.

Going to Conferences

23. Go to the right conference.

Your time and other resources are limited, so make sure you choose your conferences wisely. Look at the list of papers you are currently reading and see if any of them are from conference proceedings — that would probably be an appropriate conference. Look at the keynote speakers that are presenting at your shortlist of conferences — are any of them authors of the papers you have been reading? Make sure you get advice from your supervisor. Talk to other students to get ideas and find out if any of them have attended conferences before. First hand accounts of past conferences should never be considered as definitive evidence on the quality, or appropriateness, of a future one of the same series, but it will give you some idea of the kind at atmosphere and the opportunities that might be available.

24. Don't be seduced by the location…

…as sometimes the best locations don't make the best conferences. I've been to some conferences in beautiful tourist cities or by the beach, and they can be great fun, but you will find it much harder to find people as they are all off having fun too.

25. After you have decided on a conference, be strategic.

If you are going to invest time and budget (indeed, perhaps some of your own money) into this conference, then you want to make sure it is really worthwhile. That will usually mean one or more of the following:

a) **Look at the list of talks** and plan out your time so that you attend the most relevant talks (especially if there are parallel sessions). If there is a bunch of you going to the same conference, conspire to make sure that any important talks that are taking place simultaneously are attended by at least one of you.

b) **Look at the list of speakers** and identify which ones you want to meet. This could be for general networking, or you may be specifically looking for some collaborative opportunity, or the sharing of some tangible benefits like data or software or copies of papers. You may also be looking to meet up with people with whom you might like to gain employment at some point in the future. Check Linkedin or Research Gate to see if any of them are connected to your supervisor and if so, ask for a quick email introduction *before* the conference. Some of these people might be very obviously your "senior", both in terms of academic standing as well as age, so check with Section 29 for practical tips on how to actually introduce yourself to these people.

c) **Talk a strategy through with your supervisor.** It may surprise you to learn that some of your international peers are not the most approachable of people. Get first hand advice from your supervisor on who is easy to talk to, how to approach them, what to talk about, and what to ask them.

26. Finding funding.

Finding financial support for your conference trip can be a challenge. There are many organisations that can give you small amounts of money to attend conferences (sometimes only if you are presenting a paper or a poster) and you might have to put some effort in to finding the ones that are appropriate. Don't be shy about asking your supervisor for a contribution, especially if their name is on the paper (the worst that can happen is that they will say no). Many academic or professional societies have schemes to support students attending conferences — all you have to do is become a member. A student membership fee is normally extremely low (they want to get you involved early!) so you might find that it costs you $20 to join, but you can immediately bid for $200 towards your conference attendance.

27. Once you are there, meet people.

As many as you can— the social elements of a conference are arguably the most important part because that is where the conversations, discussions and debates happen, so make the most of the opportunities. Go to dinner. If nobody invites you, then invite yourself into some other group. It's both a bit lame, and a waste of good work time, to eat on your own. If you are with people from your own institution, or with someone you already know then it's a bit easier. If you are on your own, your mission should be to find someone to eat with. Large groups are best — its less creepy to join a group of people that you don't know than it is to ask a random individual to dinner! The best bet is to get talking to some people as part of a group just as the day's sessions are ending. Use the hints for small talk (29) if you have difficulty with this. Then, at an opportune moment, you ask, "So, are you guys going somewhere for dinner? Is it OK if I join you?" Don't worry, this is a self-selecting process. The people that you are most likely to have an enjoyable evening with are also the ones most likely to welcome you into their group of diners. If they don't, then you might want to reconsider whether they are really the kind of people you'd want to spend an evening with.

Notice that I assumed that the member of the bigger group didn't take it upon themselves to invite you. Let that be a lesson — some day it may be you who are in the big group and you might notice a lonely PhD student chatting to someone in your group just before it is time to eat (timing can be culturally specific, of course) so INVITE THEM! Don't wait for them to ask. That makes it so much easier for everyone.

28. I would tend to avoid groups that start to grow beyond 12 members.

You have to weigh up the pros and cons yourself,

but groups that get to 15 or more start to become unwieldy and very slow, especially if there is not a strong figure, or 2 or 3 figures, who will take the lead and make decisions. The primary decision is where to eat and that can be a surprisingly long process. As a PhD student I remember wandering aimlessly with a large group of conference attendees, progressively bypassing restaurants because they didn't meet some criteria. "I don't like Chinese." "We had pizza last night." etc. The size of the group needn't always be the deciding factor here, as a small group sometimes expects more of a consensus whereas members of a very large group generally recognise that not everyone will be satisfied — a group of 6 might believe that it's possible to find a compromise that suits all. If no leadership figure emerges to make the decision before everyone starves to death, then step forward and be that decision maker… or make your excuses and slink off to eat on your own.

29. Agree the bill up front.

Aim to make everyone agree up front what the situation will be when it comes time to paying the bill. I remember attending a conference in San Francisco where a bunch of old professors ate big steaks and side orders and plenty of wine, while a few PhD students went for soup and bread so as not to break their measly daily budget. The bill came and the profs went, "Oh, that's easy, we can just split it X ways." The poor PhD students were too intimidated to speak up. Don't let that happen to you (and when, in the future, it is you who is the professor, don't do it to other PhD students!).

30. Some tips for small talk.

Some people have a natural gift when it comes to small talk. Others, need some help. I once heard about a mnemonic for people doing cold-reading (the art of faking things like mind reading, palm reading, clairvoyance, etc) and I remembered it (perhaps incorrectly) as a "Rule of Thumbs", whereby THUMBS helped remember the topics that sitters want to hear in this context: Travel, Health, the Unexpected, Money, Sex (relationships). I don't recall what the "B" was for. As long as you covered all these topics in your made-up fortune telling, people were generally happy. I made up another one for small-talk. RAFT. It's a lifesaver. I could have chosen another acronym from these letters, but this one seems more appropriate somehow. It stands for Research, Ambitions, Funding, Travel. Some examples: Research. *Have you got any publications coming out? Are you publishing the work you presented this week?* Ambitions. *What are you going to do when you finish your PhD? When did you realise you wanted to be X* (the job the person is currently in). Funding. *How are you for funding right now? Are you preparing any grants? Who funded the research you presented?* Travel. *How did you get to the conference? Have you been anywhere else lately? What was your favourite location for a conference?* If you try all of these and a natural conversation doesn't start to evolve beyond the formulaic, then go speak to someone else.

Oral Presentation

31. Golden rules.

There are three golden rules that you must obey at a conference presentation more than any other.

- Stick to time.

- Don't overrun.

- Finish within the allotted time.

The only thing less professional and more likely to really annoy your audience than you running over time, is a session moderator who lets you. You might ask, "Is it OK to run over just a minute or two?" No. Just don't run over. It is that simple. Have I ever over-run? Of course I have, but the motto of this book is do as I say, not as I do! The fact that I've slipped into unprofessionalism in my time is because I didn't use the following tips to ensure I get it right:

a) **Practice**. If you practice your talk, ideally in front of your colleagues prior to departing for the event, you are more likely to keep to your allotted time (remembering to leave time for questions).

b) **Remember to speak slowly.** Better to say less, but well-rehearsed and perfectly timed, than trying to cram it all in. Take a few deep breaths before you start, and when you start speaking, remember that your speaking always sounds much, much slower to you than it does to the audience. You are probably still speaking too fast if it does not sound painfully slow to you.

c) There is a rule of thumb that you should have **one slide per minute** of talking. I'd urge caution on that one, as it depends on the nature of the slides (sometimes I effectively have one slide but because of animations it may look like quite a few, and certainly takes more than a minute to present). Certainly if you find you have 50% more slides than minutes allocated, then you need to practice and double check it works. If you have more than twice as many slides as minutes, you definitely have too many - you audience won't keep up.

d) **The moderator of the session is your *backup* for time keeping**. They should give you an indicator of when your time is running out. If he/she doesn't inform you beforehand about their mechanism for letting you know about this, ask them.

e) If you are using some kind of presentation software, the best option for time keeping is to **use a presenter-view with your slides**. Annoyingly many conferences and presentation rooms have the projector set up simply to mirror the presenter's screen, rather than as a separate monitor. Some laptops (ie, Macs) and some tablets will automatically assume a connected projector is a second screen, so when you start your presentation what you will see is the presenter-view showing the current slide, the next slide, any presenter notes and the time elapsed (or just the time). Meanwhile the audience only sees the current slide projected onto the screen. This is very useful in lots of ways (e.g. it allows you to make a good link through to the next slide) but it will also help you keep time.

f) It should go without saying that **your slides should be of good quality**. Attend a course or find a book or a website with tips on good slides. Keep them simple. Minimise the amount of text. Make the text that is there big enough. All those kinds of basics.

g) **Be yourself.** Find out who you are, your personality, and use it to make your presentation more interesting. I am sure your work is very interesting, but the slides themselves won't bring the work to life. It is you, with your personality, humour, enthusiasm, endeavour, courage, warmth, like-ability. It is these things that will persuade your audience to pay attention. It is these things that are most likely to get you a job.

h) **Ask a friend or colleague** to use their phone to video you presenting, either in the rehearsal or at the actual event. Review it and note down what you think works and what doesn't. See if that tallies with what your friends/colleagues think. It is the most effective way to learn how to be better. It will feel a bit awkward at first, but it is worth it in the end, because you will become a much better public speaker.

i) **Present as often as you can.** Take every opportunity to volunteer to give talks. If giving talks is something that you dislike or it makes you feel uncomfortable, then all the more reason to do it again, and again. The only way for you to improve — the only way to achieve the confidence necessary to make it feel less uncomfortable — is to do it over and over again. Each time aim to improve one small element of your presentation: maybe one time focus on improving your engagement with the audience; on another, focus on getting the slides right. Review your own performance each time (most easy to do if someone has videoed your presentation) and identify what might be improved.

Conference Dinners

32. There is one important overarching tip about conference dinners...

… make sure you are sitting with the right people. You are free to define "right" any way you want. It may be friends or colleagues, new or old. Just having an enjoyable evening with colleagues is valuable in itself. They may be people you have identified as potential collaborators, or future employers, or just someone whose work you have admired and want to know more about. The challenge is getting yourself at the same table.

Round tables are always the best — nobody is put at a disadvantage. Being at the end of a rectangular table is a distinct disadvantage as it limits the number of different conversations you can join. When deciding where to sit at any given conference table, try to imagine which seat will give you the greater choice of conversations. Giving yourself choice is the key to having an enjoyable dinner.

33. If you are feeling confident, once everyone is settled, you might like to lead on some ice breakers for your table.

Ice-breakers are good because (a) you want people to talk to each other and make new friends/connections, and (b) you all want to have a good time. The following ideas are good for tables of people who don't know each other too well.

> - Ask everyone to introduce their neighbour. This can work in pairs, where each person introduces one person next to them, and then they reciprocate. You will need an even number.

> - Ask everyone to think of three things about themselves (perhaps the kind of thing they might put on a CV, or in a bio) to tell the rest of the table. The catch is that two of them should be true, but one of them must be false. The rest of the table then has to guess which one is the lie.

34. Don't drink too much.

As a student, the temptation of free booze is often too much to resist. I know, I have been there. But if you can, it's a good idea to resist. If you really can't resist, here are some important other pointers: Pace yourself to match the group you are with. You can get away with being drunk at a conference event (or afterwards in the pub) as long as you are not the *most* drunk.

If you are with a group that don't drink, don't drink. If your table has some others that are having a pint from the bar before dinner, then you can join them, but don't be the only one with a pint. If everyone is drinking wine, top up other people's glasses before your own (which is a common courtesy anyway, so there is definitely no reason not to do this). Don't top yours up if nobody else is topping up. If everyone at your table is really getting into the party spirit, then make sure you ask the waiting staff if there are any more complimentary bottles of wine before the other tables do! Seriously, there are always extra bottles budgeted for in the conference dinner, and so ask the staff. If you have exercised common courtesies to the staff throughout the evening (speaking to them, saying thank you, looking them in the eye instead of ignoring them, etc, etc) then they will be predisposed to help you out. The worst that can happen is that they say "no" (and then it is only because some other tables asked before you did).

35. One final tip for conferences.

When you visit the toilet, **dry your hands thoroughly**. I mean *really* thoroughly. Not that quick flip-flap under the hand drier, but a thorough drying until a delicate paper towel wouldn't show even the tiniest spot. Why? Because one day (and this applies especially to men) you'll meet someone important just as you leave the toilet and you'll need to shake their hand. Believe me, simply saying, "Oh, don't worry, its only water, I didn't just piss all over my hands," is not the best way to introduce yourself to a senior peer (no pun intended).

Poster Presentation

36. Posters are not papers.

I saw a poster once, at a huge conference in San Francisco, which was simply the four printed A4 sheets of the conference paper pinned to the board. It was most probably because they had lost their actual poster en route, but it did bring into clear focus for me, as a young PhD candidate, that a poster is very, very different. So, what makes a good poster? Here are my four criteria for a good poster.

a) **Catch the eye.** There should be much more to the poster than simply being eye-catching, but if nobody ever stops to look at your poster, then how will they find out about the exciting work you've been doing. There is one simple thing you can do to attract the human eye — add a picture of a human face. It may be of you doing fieldwork, or a picture of the authorship team, or the lab team, or simply a mug-shot of you to identify you as the author. Human faces are the one thing human perception can't resist.

b) **Have a clear message.** Decide on a straightforward story to tell and present the evidence concisely. Your audience is only going to remember three things about your poster. One of those, you hope, is your name or institution (so make sure your name and contact details are very clear). That only leaves two things. Make sure one of them is the key conclusion of the work you are presenting — make it part of the title and make it clearly the conclusion. Everything else in the poster is then only background explanation for why you drew that conclusion.

c) **Navigation**. Make sure your audience can find their way around your poster. Good navigation is determined by the layout. Use a non-linear approach but aim to achieve a layout that follows the natural movement of human attention: i.e.. humans tend to start in the middle, 1/3 of the way down from the top, then browse upwards, then broadly speaking they go from top left to bottom right (although this may apply more to cultures with latin-language structure). Above all, aim to keep it simple. It is also more pleasing on the eye if poster elements (figures, blocks of text, images) have a sense of rhythm — keep them within a narrow range of styles (size, shape and colour) and maintain similar spaces between them. Align edges or centres across all the elements.

d) **Think carefully about the way you display data**. I recommend taking a look at the books by Edward Tufte which pretty much tell you everything you need to know about good data graphics.

e) **Legibility**. Effective navigation is important, but it is vital that your text is legible and is written in simple statements to ease comprehension. Use an appropriate font (and keep the same one throughout). Think carefully about how you justify your text. The justification of block text has a big impact on readability. It is generally recommended that for block text you justify one side only (with left justification being easier to read than right). This allows the reader to more easily trace their path through the text. This is particularly important for sans serif fonts. Full justification often makes a bolder design element and can make your poster more aesthetically pleasing, but be careful you don't sacrifice readability. The ideal width of block text is usually between 30 and 70 character spaces, with 66 often cited as the optimum. The font and line spacing will have an impact on readability also. Text that is too wide (more than 80 character spaces) is difficult to read because it is difficult to keep your place. Text that is too narrow (less than 30) never lets you get into the flow of the text and is distracting. Consider the spacing between the lines.

f) **Colours**. Tests show that the best legibility for block text is black type on a white background. This is probably because we are so used to using ink on paper, and humans find it easier to perceive the presence of things, rather than their absence. Historically it was also related to printing limitations. White on a dark background has a great visual impact, and you can probably get away with it for small amounts of text (but don't use tiring colours like red). For heading text, you can generally get away with anything, within reason.

g) **Use text hierarchies**. The term "hierarchy" refers to the layers of information and the relative emphasis you place on them. Title-subtitle-text is one example of a simple text hierarchy. You can use the size, weight or tone of a font to let the audience know which is the most important (or least important) text.

h) **Reward your audience.** Think carefully about the context in which your poster will be viewed. Will it be at a workshop in a small room with an audience composed of a small number of experts? Or is it a large international conference, where your poster has to compete for attention with a thousand other posters? What will your audience value? If it's the former, you can be more technical and provide details. For the latter you need the poster to be more attention-seeking and it must convey a clear message that a viewer will quickly comprehend. A poster that will be read without you there will require special attention to its comprehension.

37. Watch my Prezi.

I made a short Prezi on poster design for students at my institution. You can find it here: **http://prezi.com/knlu5ybepqc6/** or by searching for "The Art of the Scientific Poster"

Writing your thesis

38. Start writing as soon as you start your PhD.

The earlier you start, the easier it will be. Most universities will try to get you to do some writing very early on in the process — probably a literature review or some kind of progress report. Write these documents as if they will one day form part of your final thesis. Put them into some kind of broader structure, rather than considering them as stand-alone documents. Sketch out your chapter headings as soon as you feel comfortable with you topic, and set up a master document with these chapters. Populate this master document as you go along. It will change, evolve, adapt to circumstances, of course. But it is often easier to evolve develop and expand an existing document you have been working with as you go along than it is to start completely from scratch (which will seem like a very big hill to climb after 2+ years of research).

39. Write a conference paper at every opportunity.

It is best to attend conferences that have paper submissions that go along with oral presentations. Some of the very best conferences won't do that, and I'm not suggesting you don't attend those conferences, but attending events that give you deadlines for submitting something tangible is a good way to force you to start writing things down.

40. Back up (and often).

Never have only one version of your thesis for longer than about a week. Always back up your work, and make sure it is stored in a separate location from your working version. There is no harm in even printing a paper copy now and then, partly to keep checking your formatting and your figures, but also as a backup.

Getting Started on the Thesis

Structure

41. Tell a story

Like all good story telling (and a thesis is just that – telling the story of your research) a thesis should have a well-thought-out structure. Don't underestimate the importance of this, since a thesis that has a solid structure is one that is easier to write, easier to add to and most importantly, from the point of view of the examiner, is easier to read.

The most common structure goes at least as far back as Aristotle: beginning, middle and end. The boundaries between them are not always perfectly defined, but the steady progression should always be apparent. Consider a book, or a play or a movie that you like, and you'll notice that they will generally follow this straightforward structure with common elements to each part. Here is how Aristotle explains it in his *Poetics*: "A whole is that which has a beginning, a middle, and an end. A beginning is that which does not itself follow anything by causal necessity, but after which something naturally is or comes to be. An end, on the contrary, is that which itself naturally follows some other thing, either by necessity, or as a rule, but has nothing following it. A middle is that which follows something as some other thing follows it. A well-constructed plot, therefore, must neither begin nor end at haphazard, but conform to these principles." Put simply: The Beginning assumes nothing. The End ties up all the loose ends. The Middle takes what was given in the Beginning and leads you through the story.

The Beginning

42. Put some effort into the Introduction.

The Introduction is possibly the most important chapter of a thesis – as is the opening of any story: the first chapter of a book, the first few scenes of a movie. At the beginning, a number of things must be done – we must set the scene. The main characters are introduced. They are put into some kind of context of time and place, and some indicators are given as to what will happen in the main bulk of the story. The plot need not be given away entirely, but all the information we need to know to follow the story should be presented at the beginning. Typically, within the first few minutes of a movie we know what the rest of it is going to be like – a love story or a thriller or a horror movie. An introduction should also present the reasons for the study, where you expected it to lead to and your rationale for the approach taken. The introduction need not summarise the results, but it should allude to where the thesis eventually ends up.

In the same way, your thesis must introduce the main players in the first couple of chapters – the topics that will be relevant to the research story – and put them into the context of the wider subject matter through a thorough but well focused and concise reflection of previous work on this topic. I avoid calling this a "literature review" since you are not so much reviewing the literature in its entirety, but narrowly reflecting upon the literature (which can be formal or informal) that specifically relates to your thesis (and not necessarily the entire subject area).

43. Don't finish the Introduction until the rest of the thesis is finished.

Writing your thesis should be an iterative, non-linear process. You will not start with the first sentence, write all the middle sections, then end with the last sentence. You will lay out a structure, plan headings, modify, add extra material, rearrange, adjust. As part of that process, your concluding chapter and your introductory chapter are dependent on all the other chapters, so they should be finalised last. And the Introduction probably last of all.

Middle

44. Add some substance

When the scene is set, and the characters introduced, we come to real substance of the story.

This is where interesting things happen, the plot unfolds and the characters actually do something – they interact, rather than simply being isolated characters. In your thesis, the main body of the text is about what you did, how you did it, why you did it like *this* and not like *that*, and so on.

45. Don't try to pad it out

It does, of course, include your results, but don't be tempted to pad the thing out with results. Make sure you use succinct, concise and efficient ways of representing the data. Select those results that are relevant to the discussion – large sets of results can be summarised statistically, without having to present multiple data sets that don't add to the flow of the thesis. But don't simply select all the good ones!! Results that are contrary to a theory or expectation are important – they are the ones most likely to tell you something interesting (ie, something you didn't know already). And by convincingly explaining such results you both contribute to your main arguments (because you offer up alternative scenarios but can explain them) as well as help demonstrate your understanding of the theory/experiment.

46. Above all, present your evidence in as clear and straightforward manner as possible.

To paraphrase Einstein, "Make things as simple as possible – but no simpler".

End

47. The Concluding chapter…

… (which may be entitled Conclusions, Summary, Discussion, or whatever) is probably the next most important chapter after the Introduction. These two chapters together ultimately add value to the straightforward presentation of results that make up the middle chapters. Everything that is important about your work should be gleaned from the first and last chapters. This is both good writing practice (so that published papers should be similarly structured) but it is also the case that a lazy examiner may only read (properly) these two chapters.

48. The Ending is a consequence of all that came before

In storytelling, the End captures the essence of the story, rounds off all the loose ends, and helps define the whole point of the story (".. and the moral of the story is…"). The End is a consequence of those elements that have come before. Similarly, a thesis conclusion must summarise the research, the method and the results, capturing the essence of your thesis. More than that, it must take the results and/or analysis and, by bringing together all the previous smaller conclusions made throughout the thesis, make conclusions that encompass the specific results of the thesis as well as the wider implications to the subject as a whole. Effectively, you must answer the question, "What do all these results mean?" It is not sufficient for a concluding chapter merely to summarise the content of the thesis. It should be substantive.

49. Open Endings

Another important feature of the ending, is the idea of the open ending – for movies this is often with the aim of allowing the possibility of a sequel, and we can all think of good examples. In a thesis, the open ending is to address further work. A thesis is a discrete piece of work, but research goes on forever (which sounds more profound that it really is!). It is a measure of how much you learned through doing your thesis to be able to see what you might have done differently, what you should have done differently, and what you would now do if you had a further 3 years of funding to work on the subject some more. From an examiner's point of view, it also helps to see how much you ultimately understood about the subject and the process of research. Don't ignore the gaps in your thesis, but build on them and make them the foundation of possible future work.

The Other Bits

50. Think about the add-ons.

Besides the main structure of the thesis described above, you also have to include certain add-ons, which have a bit of a life of their own and so deserve some explanation.

Abstract

51. Abstracts are important

An abstract is an odd piece of text, and it often takes some time to get used to writing them. They are strange because they give away the plot. While a good movie trailer or the back-cover summary of a novel gives you an overview of the story, it shouldn't really tell you what happens, whereas the purpose of an abstract is to do just that. It shouldn't try to "tempt" people to read the thesis (or paper) but rather concisely describe the fundamental features of the methods employed and the results obtained. It should be dry and straightforward, and give enough information that if someone only read the abstract, they would know instantly whether they wanted to read the whole text or not. If you take a look at some published papers, you'll see what I mean, although take care, as there are plenty of bad examples of abstracts out there.

Preface

52. Another funny beast.

A preface is not an introduction, nor an abstract, nor a summary. Personally, I think the preface is the place where you get to say what you want, in a manner that best suits you – write more informally, and feel free to express your own opinions. It is perhaps the only part of a thesis where you can express your own personality without condemnation – no one is likely to (nor should they) fail a thesis on a bad preface!

53. Usually a preface begins with some interesting personal reflections on the thesis topic and the very wide and historical context of the subject.

This then leads to a summary, chapter by chapter, of the contents, and a quick summary of why the thesis might be important. It is often appropriate to include acknowledgements here, but putting them in their own slot after the preface is also acceptable.

Appendices

54. Add all the extra stuff that hasn't been used already, but only if useful.

All the stuff that has not been published in a paper, nor in the main body of the thesis, but would be useful for the reader (or examiner) to refer to: software code, proofs, interesting sideline studies that you have done that are not directly relevant to the thesis topic, or would disrupt the natural flow of the main text. Include here extensive data sets, extended interview transcripts, additional results and glossaries or lists of symbols. Do not fill this up with material to make an otherwise thin-looking thesis look more substantial — most examiners see through that old trick. Only included material that is genuinely useful.

55. Reprints

It is also acceptable to include reprints of papers that you have published during your thesis as appendices, but only if they are relevant.

Footnotes and Endnotes

56. The use of footnotes and endnotes are ultimately a matter of opinion.

In general, if something needs extra explanation, or elucidation, but to do so in the main body of the text would interrupt the flow, or main thrust of an argument, then a *note* is a good idea. Whether these should be footnotes or endnotes will be determined by the official formatting guidelines set out by your institution.

Postscripts and Afterwords

57. These are effectively the equivalent of the Preface...

...but they come after the main body of the text. In general, anything that could be included here should have been dealt with earlier in the thesis. They should really only be included if there is something that turns up at the very last minute – too late to change the text of the thesis. You may, for instance, want to (or be asked to) add a Postscript or

Afterword after your viva if there were significant comments made by your examiner that would contribute to the thesis as a whole. The other rare occasion would be that some new piece of research is published between the time of your first submission and your viva – you might then wish to add an Afterword before binding your thesis to make reference to the new work, and how it ties in with your own.

General Comments

58. Cite to support your claims.

When you use terms like "Many authors have said…" then make sure that is followed by plenty of citations. Likewise, be careful about how much you "assume". You are immersed in this topic, but your audience may not be. So make sure you back up all your initial claims with appropriate citations or explanations.

59. Be SMART.

If you use SMART words throughout your thesis, you will avoid being too general, too vague or imprecise. For example, when wording your aims and objectives, there are some words that convey the journey and other words that emphasise the result. The following are a list of what might be considered as "journey" words (and note that this list is not exhaustive),

Journey words:

- Study
- Analyse
- Enquire
- Explore
- Investigate
- Look at
- Examine

These words are non-SMART – they are not specific and cannot be measured (meaning that you cannot tell when it is completed). They imply process, not results. They are about how you intend to do something, not what you will end up with at the end. There is nothing wrong with these words – you will do many of these things in the process of achieving your result. The problem is that if you are claiming an aim, or an objective, these words make for less compelling statements, and are much harder to refer back to in your conclusions.

Instead, here are some "result" words (again, not an exhaustive list):

- Test (a hypothesis)
- Evaluate (a method)
- Quantify (a relationship)
- Establish (a connection)
- Verify
- Understand
- Answer
- Find

- Enable
- Provide
- Create
- Gain insight into

These words imply a result. They might also describe a process, but they are result-focussed. They are SMART because you can tell if you have achieved it or not. It is very easy to say that you will study X or investigate Y, but it is not at all clear when that task has been completed. You can *study* something for a lifetime, or you could *study* it for an afternoon. To say you will *find* some property of X, or that you aim to *understand* how Y works, sets a clearer boundary to the task. You either achieve it, or you don't. That makes it much more SMART, and as a result, it makes writing your concluding chapters much easier — it is much easier to refer back to SMART aims and explain how you have achieved them.

Size Does Matter

60. In a thesis, size does matter.

A thesis can be too short or too long, but unfortunately there is no absolute standard to determine this. The length will depend more upon the subject and your style of writing, than upon how much actual work you do. Examiners are never fooled into thinking that a big thesis means you did lots of work.

61. Rough guides.

As a rough guide, for single-sided, double-spaced, A4, you would expect a 6-month MSc project to produce a thesis about 50-80 pages long. A 12-month research MSc thesis, a little longer, say, 70-100. A PhD, from about 100-200. (For 4 year PhDs it could be as much as 300, but 180-250 is probably more realistic in most cases). Large Appendices may bring these numbers up a little.

62. When it starts becoming two volumes, it is probably too big.

You should be able to be focused and concise, and so keep it under 250 pages, max. A two volume MSc thesis should, in my opinion, be asked to re-submit without even looking at the text. I did see one such thesis once, which contained a series of photos along the lines of, "Fig 1. About to dig some soil samples", "Fig. 2. Digging some soil samples." "Fig. 3. A soil sample is put in a bag"… etc. Each photo took up a single page!

Remember, a 4-page published paper may describe the equivalent of many months, or even years, of work. There is no reason why your thesis shouldn't be equally focused and concise.

Writer's Block

It is all very well me giving tips on how to write a thesis, but often the hardest thing is just getting started in the first place. Here are some tips to overcome writer's block.

63. Start small.

Focus on some key elements of your work. Can
you summarise your thesis in one sentence? Or at
least in one paragraph? Compressing your thesis
into a short, succinct summary is a good discipline
to practice. Once you have tried very short
summaries, try doing it on a single side of paper.
The top third should be a background or context.
The bottom third your conclusions, bullet pointed if
that helps. Then fill the middle with a summary of
the evidence that justified your conclusions. If you
find this difficult, then good — it means you are on
your way to writing your thesis because you will
start to realise that before justifying your
conclusions you need to explain more about X and
Y. And then you will realise that your introduction
needs to be expanded to include justifications and
explanations of what has been done to date. Keep
expanding.

64. Mind map.

Often I find that one of the biggest blocks to getting
started is not getting the story right — not knowing
where to start, nor where it ends, and not really
knowing the path in-between as well. A common
problem I have seen is when you are comparing
multiple methods, ideas or approaches: say you are
trying to compare A, B and C, and each one has
three components, (i), (ii) and (iii). How do I write
this up? Do I do it like this:

Chapter 3: A (i), (ii), (iii)

Chapter 4: B (i), (ii), (iii)

Chapter 5: C (i), (ii), (iii)

Or do I structure it like this:

Chapter 3: A (i), B (i), C (i)

Chapter 4: A (ii), B (ii), C (ii)

Chapter 5: A (iii), B (iii), C (iii)

There is no correct way to do this, only effective ways and ineffective ways. For your particular topic one way might work better than another. In all cases, mind mapping should help with this as it breaks up the linear structure that is imposed upon the topic by thinking about writing. Mind maps, sometimes known as radial maps or spider diagrams, are non-linear — there is no beginning, middle and end. There are just hierarchical connections. Breaking the linearity will help you to see connections that maybe weren't apparent before, and will offer a new way to look at the material you have to cover. Here are some tips to get started on mind mapping:

a) Gather together some coloured pens. Drawing pictures and using multiple colours helps stimulate the mind in different ways from simply writing words all the time.

b) Start in the centre with an image that represents the topic of your thesis (or question or aim) or write the words very large, in colour, with an elaborate style.

c) Write some other topics or words that are connected to the main topic and connect them to the centre with a line. Some methods for mind mapping vary as to whether you label the line or the node (where lines meet). My preference is to use the nodes for nouns or static topics, whereas the lines I label with verbs, or actions or processes (the process that takes you from one node to the next).

d) Keep adding new words and lines connecting them. All lines should link back to the centre. You can "code" your map with a hierarchy so that broader titles or topics have larger text and thicker lines, and typically these words will be near the centre. Getting to finer granularity, or greater sub-sub-sub-topics, the text gets smaller, the lines get thinner.

e) Practice often so that you develop your own personal style of mind mapping.

f) Make links across any parts of the map that are connected. This risks getting messy, but does start to draw out connections that you might not have thought about before. If you get too many connections that cross the general radial pattern, then consider starting again, but this time putting some topics in different locations to make the final map look more organised.

Once you have done some mind mapping, revisit the tasks (a)-(f) above and see if you can construct a clearer structure that tells a coherent story. (There are plenty of free software packages for doing mind maps. My favourite is Cmaps, simply because it allows me to label both the connecting lines and the nodes, which seems to be a rare feature.)

65. Randomise.

If the two tasks above don't work, try randomising your work instead. This is a classic tool used by creative types and psychologists to disrupt particular patterns of thinking. If you have got yourself into a rut trying to make sense of your thesis and simply don't know where to start any more, then try this: Write all the key elements of your thesis on separate pieces of paper. Make them SMART — so, don't write "methodology" on a piece of paper, but rather the actual name of your particular methodology or methodological approach. If you can bullet point some conclusions, then add them each to a piece of paper. If you have some key results, put them on individual pieces. If you have some key results in the form or diagrams or graphs, then have them too. Eventually you should have a pile of pieces of paper that list topics, or would-be sections, or sub-sections, or figures, etc. (You can also use the same approach by taking a conference paper, or your mind map, or your single page thesis summary and then cutting it up into pieces). Then make some space on a large table, or on the floor, and throw them all in the air (or, alternatively, turn them face down on a table and then mix them up, then turn them over). Now try to bring them all together in a linear format that makes sense, either individually by selecting pieces of paper one by one, or by grouping the paper into relevant piles. Once you are finished, remember to keep a record of the result.

Don't Write Forever

66. Read your work.

Always factor in time to read your own work and have it read by others. The proofreading is important to ensure not only that the text is readable, but that it flows correctly in a logical order — that that story and the argument makes sense. You may get friends or relatives or colleagues to read individual chapters as you go along, but always ensure someone reads an early draft of the entire thesis, from beginning-to-end. Your supervisor is someone who will also want to do this (at least they *should*) but your supervisor knows the subject and is so focused on the content that they may not be the best person for spotting errors in the story-telling. You will also want to read it beginning-to-end yourself, but I would typically suggest doing this after taking some time away from it. Re-reading after returning after a week or two holiday, for instance, will give you a fresh perspective, so remember to factor that in to your planning.

67. Stop.

While at the start it may be writer's block that hinders you from completing your thesis, you may find that near the end the opposite is true —that you can't stop writing. You may find that when you finally get your first draft of your thesis together, you decide you want to re-write the first couple of chapters. This is an important and valuable iterative process, but be careful that you do not continue this ad infinitum. What can happen is that you spend another couple of months doing those chapters, which gives you enough time to start questioning the latter chapters. So you decide to spend a further couple of months doing them… by which time, the introductory chapters are starting to look a bit out of date again… and so on, until you are 12 months behind schedule. Remember, your thesis does not need to be *absolutely* perfect. At some point you need to decide that it is time to stop.

It's a positive thing to want to produce the best thesis possible, but a late thesis is always a bad thing. In 10, 20 years time, when people are looking are your career record they'll see the 12 month delay before they ever see the actual thesis. A PhD thesis is not just about the work itself, but is also about how you do it, and about completing the work within a reasonable time period.

Figures

68. Use photographs.

If you can find a good reason to add them, include some photos in your thesis. Photos of people or places are especially good — they add a bit of colour, literally, to your thesis and makes it much more fun for your examiner.

69. Think carefully about how you display your data.

If you are representing data, make sure you have thought carefully about the visualisation of your data. The books by Edward Tufte (also recommended in (36)) on data visualisation will help you think carefully about the way in which you are using visuals to communicate your data.

70. Be generous with your figure captions.

Make them fully self-explanatory so that your reader not only gets a description of what the figure contains, but also some insight into what it is telling you. If there is something worth highlighting, then do so in the caption.

71. Print high quality.

Colour pictures can cause a lot of hassle if you do not have easy access to a (cheap) colour laser printer. Alternatively, print good quality versions for the submitted thesis on the best printer you can find (or have them done commercially). Do them on a single page each, without a page number. This way, if the text on a previous page is changed, you don't have to re-print an expensive glossy print.

72. Don't be lazy with your data graphics.

The ease with which you can now generate colour plots has tended to make researchers lazy with their graphics. Colour is not always the easiest way to display some results or data – sometimes colour is added as a poor substitute for thinking about how best to display the results. Always think twice about how you represent data and ideas, especially if you are footing the bill for the colour laser prints!

Peer Reviewed Journal Articles

73. Whenever possible, write a journal article.

Why? Because a published article in a respected peer-reviewed journal is still the Gold Star of academic achievement. Some institutions will allow you to compile your thesis based on a set of publications, and indeed, some supervisors will insist on you doing so. It should be discussed with your supervisor, with reference to your institution's rules and regulations, before you decide whether this is a good path for you to follow. But thesis aside, if there is a chance to publish some of your results, then definitely invest the time and energy into that. If for no other reason than because it will stand you in good stead when it comes to post-PhD job hunting. Note that the peer-reviewed articles are especially important because it means your work has been scrutinised by scholars in your field and deemed acceptable. Such a gate-keeper process validates what you have done, and will help reassure you that the work you are doing is of sufficient quality. Be wary, though, of the rise of the spurious open-access-journal-scam. Online open access journals are popping up everywhere and there is a good chance that you will at some point receive an email from one inviting you to submit an article. Unless it is a reputable journal that your supervisor has vetted, then don't submit anything. Delete the email. Avoid like the plague. The way the scam works is that within weeks they will get back to you to let you know your paper was peer reviewed and has been accepted for publication. They will then ask you for $500 (or similar) for the author publishing fee (a common request even amongst the reputable open access journals). I dare not imagine how many researchers have been suckered into paying the fee.

74. A thesis in miniature.

When writing a good scientific paper, you can follow all the same ideas as outlined above for your thesis. It is, after all, a bit like a thesis in miniature. There is one important difference, though, which is that a paper is not for examining the authors. In this sense, it should be more concise. It can assume a greater knowledge on the part of the reader (as you are not trying to convince that reader of what you know). And the ability to be very focused with your results and conclusions is even more important.

75. Ask yourself: What is the purpose of this paper?

Unfortunately, the desire (need?) to get work published often clouds the issue of this question. In some respects, a paper should allow repeatability – you must give enough information that the reader can come to the same conclusions. In this context it also needs to be convincing! It should also be a source for authors to find other good literature on the subject.

76. Above all, it must communicate.

It should communicate your ideas, your theories, a

set of results and your understanding of them. If it doesn't communicate your work and insights to the reader, then it is ultimately worthless.

77. Find inspiration

When you plan to write your first paper, my advice is to choose a published paper that you liked and enjoyed reading (and was preferably also quite logical and straightforward) and … well, don't copy it, but do use it for inspiration. Use it to guide your style, the level of the content and the structure. It's the best way to learn.

Checklist

Here is a final checklist for your almost-finished thesis. Ask yourself the following questions:

About the content…

78. Understanding the topic:

Have I shown that I understand the topic of the thesis? Is there anything in the thesis that looks like I am covering up a lack of knowledge?

79. Understanding of the wider context of the research:

Do I know the relevance of this work within the wider aspects of the subject, and to other topics? And have I conveyed that in the Introduction and Conclusion?

80. Existing literature:

Does my introduction give a good overview of the recent work done on the same subject? Do I also cite the older, but classic, texts? Do I make proper use of citing other work throughout the thesis? Have I ovcr-cited – ie, cited every possible text? Have I cited anything that I have never actually seen (a bad idea)?

81. Logical reasoning and analytical ability:

Does my thesis convey a logical processes of reasoning, deduction and inference? Are my conclusions logical and reasonable deductions from the results? Are there other alternative conclusions that could be drawn? If so, do I discuss these possibilities?

82. Critical thought:

Does my thesis highlight some of the weaknesses of previous/current research? Do I consider the weaknesses of my own approach? Have I sufficiently taken into account those weaknesses when making my conclusions?

83. Further work:

Do my conclusions include a discussion of where the research should go next? Does this include identifying the shortcomings in the thesis, and how they could be improved, as well as seeing the possibilities of additional research?

84. Has your supervisor seen your entire thesis?

It might not have been a completely final version, but it is important that it has been read as an entire document and not as small discrete units.

About the presentation...

85. Structure:

Is the structure of my thesis logical? (i.e. beginning, middle, end)? Have I cluttered up the text with things that could go in an Appendix (such as software code, or reams of results that add nothing to the understanding of the thesis)? Is it too long? (Examiners don't like long theses... and it implies you can't be concise.)

86. Presentation:

Does it look good? (It needn't be a work of art, but it should look professional). Have I followed the official guidelines on format, etc?

87. Graphics and data presentation:

Do my figures and graphics help to illustrate a point, or communicate an idea, or do they simply look nice? Worse, do they confuse rather than clarify? Are all data plots suitably annotated so that they are clear (including indicators of scale, labelled axes, etc).

88. Use of language:

Have I run a spell checker? Has someone proofread the document to check for errors in grammar or lack of clarity? A non-expert is good for this role, especially for the abstract, introduction and conclusions, as these are the most important in terms of language, so make sure they are right. Ask this person to especially look out for words that the spell checked may have missed, such as their/there, dependent/depcndant, its/it's, to/too, etc.

89. Have I met the proper formatting requirements for my institutions?

It is important to make sure you meet the expectations for such things as page length, word count, font size, line spacing, binding, citation style, own-work declarations, appendices.

Finishing Up: The Viva Voce

The advice here is for formal *viva voce* type oral examination (common in the UK), whether in private or in public. In your own country and with you own traditions, this advice might need some reinterpretation and/or modification.

90. Prepare.

Do not assume that just because you wrote the thing that you can go into an examination and still sound like you wrote it.   The longer the time delay between you submitting it and the examination, the more this becomes a pertinent issue. So, give yourself a couple of weeks break from thinking about it, but then go back and re-read your thesis, from beginning to end.   Critique it. Make margin notes in your copy, being sure to do so on an exact copy of the version the examiner has (as there is nothing worse than trying to cross-reference thesis page numbers between different versions in the actual viva). Identify errors and spelling mistakes. Read your thesis again and critique it even harder, especially those bits that you are least confident about.   I can assure you that a good examiner will skim briskly over the parts of the thesis where you demonstrate a real command of the subject, and instead will dig deep in the places you are weakest. After my own very harrowing viva I remember my external examiner telling me that, "The point of the viva was to make sure you realised how much you still don't know."

91. Dress smartly.

It is entirely possible to pass a viva looking like you've just been out on an all-night bender. But first impressions have a tendency to be stubborn. And if you turn up shabby, and you find your examiner (whom you may know to usually look shabby at their own university) turns up looking extremely smart and formal, then you risk not looking the part, and therefore not feeling the part. 99 times out of 100, it will make no difference. If you want to take that risk, then by all means do so. Note also that there are gender and cultural specifics to what is regarded as "smart". If in doubt, ask your supervisor for advice.

92. Be curious.

Ask questions. It is OK to ask your examiners for their suggestions or advice. You can also ask them what they think needs to be done to make the work publishable. Ask their advice on where to publish. By asking them questions you make this process more like a dialogue aimed at evaluation and improvement, rather than an examination.

93. Think through what the examiners might ask.

Here are some typical questions that an examiner might ask.

- In one sentence, summarise your key conclusions.

- If you were starting afresh, what would you do differently, and why?

- What do you believe you specifically brought to this work?

- In what way does your work help your field to move forward?

- What are the key original elements?

- What would you say was your primary methodology and why did you choose this approach?

- What inspired you to choose this topic?

- How did you decide what to include and what to omit in the final version?

- What is it about the topic that interests you?

- What next? What new questions have arisen as a consequence of your work?

After: Getting a job.

94. Apply and apply often.

Do not wait until you have 100% of the qualities asked for in a job advert before applying. 70% is probably enough. It has been said that men do this more regularly than women, so if you are a woman, please take this advice especially seriously. The worst that will happen is that your application is rejected. Do not be put off by that. Good people get rejected all the time. It is also important not to hold off until you find your dream job being advertised. This is particularly true if you don't have much experience of job interviews. Aim to get in some practice with jobs that meet only 60-70% of your aspirations, and for which you might meet only 60-70% of the job description. Don't worry if it looks like a long-shot — it is up to them to decide whether you are good enough.

If you get as far as the interview stage, then you are in with a chance. You have crossed their threshold for appointment. There are now only two reasons you won't get the job. First, because you messed up the interview. Being unlikeable, unpersuasive, lacking ambition, being too boring or too excitable. Second is that one of the others beat you. As long as you are beaten fair and square, then you should congratulate yourself in getting to interview, thank your interviewers for the opportunity, congratulate the appointee (you may end up working with them at some point in the future) and then review your performance to see if it could have been better. And next time, plan out how to be better.

95. Get some intel.

Sometimes it will not be fair and square. One way in which it might not be fair is because internal candidates will get inside information — who is on the panel, what are the local internal priorities, what are the gaps in teaching. They can also easily demonstrate research links with existing staff. But there is no reason you cannot do this too. Do not be put off seeking out this information just because you are not local. Ask. Give the office a call and see if they will tell you who is on the panel. See if you can find out who the other candidates are. If you ask, then it is up to them to decide whether you are allowed to know or not, so keep asking questions until they say no. It is only *unfair* if they don't give the same information to other candidates. You might also ask for a copy of the scoring sheet that the panel will use (they usually do these days). You should see if you can call the Chair of the appointment committee and ask what they think are the priorities for the post.

Sometimes you will be asked to give a presentation, especially if it is an academic job. This will not be long enough to cover every aspect of your research and teaching, so you need to prioritise. Do this by asking the potential employer. It is entirely appropriate for you to contact people at the organisation and ask their opinion on what they believe the priorities are. Is this a very research focused position or more teaching? Do they want to hear about the past or my ideas for the future? If I could talk more about X than about Y, do you think the audience would be more interested? It is usually better to ask "either or" type questions as this does not require much thought to answer, it feels less like they are "feeding" you information, and it also doesn't look like you lack ideas. Contact some employees to ask them about their work. Arm yourself with plenty of knowledge of the company/department/organisation and who works on what. For academic teaching jobs, try to get a hold of the undergraduate teaching manual so that you can see what courses are already being offered, so that you can see where you might fit in. Ultimately, it is in your favour if the panel know your name before the interview and to consider you as "keen".

96. Ask.

You might seek third party advice on the particular institutes/job and the prospects it offers for further progress. Linkedin is a great resource to find out who in your network is already in similar jobs. I always try to connect to my students on Linkedin so that they have access to my address book for exactly this kind of thing.

97. Interview tactics.

For the actual interview itself there are also some tactics to employ. If you have to give a short presentation, then refer back to the advice above. Consider using a prop. People remember props. In the presentation for my current job, I had a model of a wave cut out of polystyrene foam board. I used it to explain why microwaves are interesting. 15 years later, some of my colleagues still remember "the wave" I used in that 20 min presentation.

Most of all, be yourself. Convey your personality (whatever kind that might be) and enthusiasm. Everyone likes an enthusiast. Know your audience. If you have met with any staff members (or employees) before the presentation, be sure to sound them out for suggestions on how to deal with the particular audience. However, be aware that they may not all be keen on the post being advertised and it is never a good idea to play with internal politics. Make copious notes beforehand. Create a table of possible questions and populate them with answers. You can take that with you. There is no restriction on what you might have in a folder in front of you. If you have done your homework properly, then you will not need it, but it is comforting to know it is there, just in case. Here are some typical questions that can get your table started (NB: these will be different for specific jobs, so use this as a starting point, not an exclusive list):

Describe the content of one of your recent published papers.

Describe the content of a recent conference paper.

Which of your publications would you consider the best?

What can you contribute to postgraduate courses?

What can you contribute to undergraduate courses?

Where are you going to get funding for your research?

If you had a PhD student start tomorrow, what topic would you have them do it on?

Your CV says you did some teaching - elaborate.

What exactly did you do when you worked at [insert name of place you worked]?

Describe your PhD project.

What would you hope to have achieved in 5 years time?

10 years?

How do you feel you would contribute to research activities in the Department? In the University?

What is it that you feel you bring to the group/company/department?

What extra funding would you need to get you started? (e.g. lab equipment, computer, specialised software, etc.)

What is your philosophy of teaching?

What do you think makes you different from the other candidates?

Do you have any other questions, or things you would like to add?

98. Give short answers that are to the point, but don't make them abrupt.

"Yes" or "no" answers are not sufficient. Panels aren't expecting really short answers like that. Suddenly finding big gaps appearing in their schedule because things are moving quicker than expected will put them ill-at-ease. You never want to make your panel feel awkward. Don't talk too long either. Pay attention to body language to get an indication if you are talking too much, and stop if you are worried, and ask, "Does that answer your question or would you like me to elaborate some more?"

99. Be you.

Don't try to modify who you are to fit with what you think they want. If you give a false impression of who you are, and they appoint you it will unravel eventually. You don't want to work in a place that doesn't value who you really are.

100. Ask questions.

Prepare a stack of questions. I always like candidates who ask questions, even ones where they have merely requested clarification on a question that had been answered at an earlier stage (or had been presented by someone already) because it shows they are actively thinking and engaging in a dialogue. The non-thinkers tend to turn up, present, thank the panel for the information and then go. Some standard questions are to do with workloads (do you really know what is expected of you in terms of your time… in the lab, doing admin, teaching, field trips, etc,?); opportunities for further development and collaboration (can I do further training in X and Y, would it be OK to collaborate with Z?); funding (is there internal funding, or grants, or other sources of internal money?);

promotion and career development (what kind of support is available for new staff to help their career progression?).   That last one is a tricky one as it may put many academic and research institutions on the spot.   If they squirm, then perhaps don't push it — it is enough of an answer if they squirm.

101. Be thankful.

After the event, drop the chair of the panel a quick email, or better still a postcard, thanking him/her for the opportunity and the organisation of his/her staff (or something positive, but true, and not obsequious). Leaving a good impression, even if you don't get the position, is always a good investment in the long term.

Afterword

A PhD is a difficult thing. It is meant to be.
Nobody would value it if it was too easy.   If I could
distil my experiences into three core bits of advice it
would be:

> - **Ask and listen**. You have two ears and
> one mouth. Use them in that proportion. A
> PhD is not a competition — people want to
> help.

> - **Plan**. Planning may not be an essential
> ingredient for success in anything, but I am
> confident that good planning always
> improves your chances of success.

> - **Persevere**. Determination to succeed,
> coupled with hard work and endeavour, will
> overcome most obstacles put in your way.
> Add this to "planning" and "asking" and you
> are well on your way to getting your PhD,
> and more.

If you found this book useful, please let me know,
and tell others.

@fortiain

i.h.woodhouse@ed.ac.uk

About the Author

Iain Woodhouse completed his own PhD in 3 years, 1 month, at Heriot-Watt University in Edinburgh in 1994. It won the Best PhD thesis award from the Remote Sensing Society. He started as a lecturer at the University of Edinburgh in 1999 and is now a Professor of Applied Earth Observation. While at Edinburgh he has supervised more than 50 MSc and 18 PhD students to a successful thesis submission. He has also acted as external examiner for a number of PhD students, both from UK universities and world-wide, including students at universities in Finland, Australia, Ghana, Canada, South Africa and the Netherlands.

Iain has also acted as an employer both within the University of Edinburgh and as a Board member of two start-up companies (Ecometrica in 2008 and Carbomap in 2013). He has had experience sitting on recruitment panels in the School of GeoSciences for appointments that have ranged from PhD student and post-doctoral researchers, to the Head of School.

Printed in Great Britain
by Amazon